Black Wall Street New Dream Publishing   THE SCIENCE OF FICTION DIALECTIC

"BEING HUMANE IS ACTIVELY SEEKING A WAY TO BUILD A RELATIONSHIP WITH HUMANITY"

David Ali Berry EL

Black Wall Street New Dream Publishing

THE SCIENCE OF FICTION DIALECTIC

David Ali Berry EL

THE SCIENCE OF FICTION DIALECTIC

DAVID ALI BERRY EL

David Ali Berry EL

Black Wall Street New Dream Publishing THE SCIENCE OF FICTION DIALECTIC

The Science of Fiction Dialectic
Copyright © 2017 By David Ali Berry EL

All rights reserved. No part of this book may be reproduced in any form or by any means without prior consent of publisher, except brief quotes used in reviews.

ISBN-13: 978-0-692-95268-9
ISBN-10: 0-692-95268-3

Author: David Ali Berry EL
Cover Design by: David Ali Berry El

Printed in the United States of America

This is a work of nonfiction. Any references or similarities to actual events, real people, living or dead, or to real locales are intended to give the novel a sense of reality. Any similarity in other names, characters, places, and incidents is entirely coincidental.

Black Wall Street New Dream Publishing
blackwallstreetnewdream@yahoo.com
David Ali Berry EL
yesusministries@gmail.com
davidthemagicnegro@gmail.com

David Ali Berry EL

Table of Contents

Abstract Warning……………………………………………………………………2

Particle 1……………………………………………………………………………**4**

Particle 2……………………………………………………………………………**7**

Particle 3……………………………………………………………………………**10**

Components of Particle 1……………………………………………………………**25**

Components of Particle 2……………………………………………………………**27**

Components of Particle 3……………………………………………………………**29**

Pictures ……………………………………………………………………………**35**

Abstract Warning:

Reading the contents will alter your land (mind) forever! If a 16-year-old American white boy named Taylor Wilson can build a nuclear reactor in his parent's garage after watching Youtube.com videos on physics, quantum mechanics and other theoretical math concepts, I can help you to rethread your brain to remind you of who you are, and what you are. You must act with (1) deliberate intellectual honesty. This means that you will be willing to eat, chew, swallow, regurgitate, and digest knowledge (in your refreshed data reticula) from some of the newest, oldest, rarest, and voluminous lexicons, dictionaries, concordances, or encyclopedias, whether the information is in digital format, written on walls, scrolls, or bindings wherever available for daily use while meditating vigorously on the contents of them all. Your internet browsers should be considered 'Oracles' from this reading forward. You must also use and (2) willfully apply empathy with prudence to perfect your discoveries. I designed the Area of Concern diagramation, along with the Toil-et Tissue diagram to solve for the 'Red Pill Quandary' of the, "Why should I concern myself with the information," question and/or quasi-rebuttal most zombified reprobates give when they are exposed as being butt ass naked to the new information they have been presented with, and are overtly ignorant about. Even a beast of a man like the planation slave owner Calvin Candie in the Django movie by Quentin Tarantino knew to ask Dr. Schultz what the definition of a word was when he didn't over stand the word's usage for himself. Are ye good, or willfully [ball and chained to] evil? Many questions remain unanswered because we let others do all the thinking for us. We allow others to ask the questions, answer the questions, and do the mental gymnastics for us. Fool me once, shame on you. Fool me twice, shame on me.

Those who have made themselves eunuchs must repent too. You are not a dry tree. The Book of Isaiah chapter LVI.3 King James Version (1599) says so. Have you ever read that chapter with your own eyes and mind yet, [gay man and lesbian woman]?

From all that I have been blessed to research and discover, I have designed this personal meme so my space-ranger brothers and sisters know why I wrote this dialectic for us.

"Being humane is actively seeking a way to build a relationship with humanity."

We are d'rugs.

Shalom bayit.

Welcome aboard: The Science of Fiction Dialectic

Graphed by Tou Sunergo con Philema, Doctor (verb form) David Ali Berry EL

Particle 1: You've Been Cruci-fictioned by the Hoodoo in You, Solamente!

The infamous pig Latin tongue, or English language was created and developed at the end of the 16th century by ambitious Machiavellian fascist white supremacist alchemist Etruscan imitating wordsmiths (body chemistry or "Spirit" pimps) with the prudence to confuse the unsuspecting, illiterate, and ignorant masses (1). English, and its many dialects, makes the comprehension of their smart word-play (especially in printed texts) nearly impossible to fully understand or comprehend unless you have an interpreter with the mental capabilities (the mind) to know the difference between divine and literal interpretations (potentiality). The 'official' or 'comforter' needed is someone who can speak and/or discern the different tongues or lenguas (Española for languages) being used aloud or printed (2,3,4).

Here's a cornbread crumb for those who can appreciate good vibrations specifically: the most misunderstood piece of the mind control rubric that is cubing our ability to discern the real magician's key to sorcery is you, the existing and eternal pneumatic human re-source, or the reprobated (5,6,7) body politic zombie brane.

Those who have claimed to have 'caught' the 'Holy Ghost' are lying to themselves, and others around them for effect (8,12,13,14). These obviously hypnotized people are experiencing self-induced psychosomatic illness or hoodoo (superstition) inspired parasympathetic nervous system manipulation (9,10). The muscle memory and mirror neuron connectivity these types of people have built up over time has caused all their 'trained' neurons to fire up (heat) simultaneously. Then hormones like dopamine and cortisol flow through the blood stream, feeding the body and brain with a quasi-hallucinogenic information deluge, complete with mindless babblings of nothingness and confusion (18). The 'Holy Ghost Catchers' often appear to seek the acceptance and approval of the congregation of fellow imitators, as well as the other confounded onlookers (10 & 11). There's no future in your fantasy, baby lion.

In response to those who mumble and babble passionately, as well as those of us whom search diligently for a reason and possible blessing hiding within this disruptive behavior, I give you this: The Prophet Paul addressed this issue in 1st Corinthians 14:19 (15; 1769AD). He said, "Yet in the church I had rather speak five words with my understanding, that *[by my voice]* I might teach others also, than ten thousand words in an *[unknown]* tongue." There are no interpreters around to translate the babble, so by default, the apelike noises, monkey grunts, and fake Hebrew word attempts that are being generated mean nothing. This activity should be banned from the re-public forever!

Today, 'officials' in Admiralty Law or Common Law courts masquerading as Civil Law courts, are called attorneys and lawyers (2,3,16,17). The British Accredited Registry baristas possess fictitious corporate state issued licenses/titles of nobility, i.e. esquire. This makes them all traitors to humanity presumably. In deed and by default, they are violating their oaths to the original Organic Constitution for the united states for America circa 1789, Al ham du li lah! Cornell University is one of the only colleges that stores/keeps records of esoteric treatises and archaic laws for our discovery. These artifacts will reveal all the hidden factoids behind how courts rule (measure) the land, esoterically known as the mind of a mankind.

2. Most People Who Tell Immigrants to Learn English Are Functionally Illiterate Themselves

The King James Version Bible and the works of William Shakespeare were some of the first works of literature published and printed in the newly created Modern English language. English is known in small cliques as a Semitic language (21,22). English is less than 500 years old. Spanish is over 1000 years old. English was created for occult and esoteric commercial purposes in my estimation. The Geneva Bible of 1560 came to the new world called America by way of the Mayflower boat, or was part of the agreement called the Mayflower Compact contract in some creatively deceptive way (23,24). The Geneva Bible is written in Early Modern English too (19). English is a language filled with serendipity and irony for those with the eyes to see, and the gears to rear the deception, to the beauty of the truth (Plato's Republic).

The King James Version Bible is ripe for syntactic analysis (25). To my knowledge, the Geneva Bible is the first time the English language plague spilled onto the shores of the North American continent. Spanish was slashing, raping, disease infecting, and prayer town establishing its way into Native American lands centuries before.

It is important to note that these early English literary works, including Shakespeare, were penned in a writing style called allegory. Allegory is the use of events, characters, and ideas to define a larger idea (28).

Music connoisseurs of rock, poetry, and rap/hip-hop, etc., have keen ears to detect the use of the writing style allegory. Allegory is like the use of metaphors and similes.

Metaphors and similes fall under the writing style called imagery. Allegory and imagery are the reasons behind why we enjoy books, plays, operas, ballets, and movies (28). Historically, allegory has been used to permit an artist or writer the 'poetic license' and protection to tell an important political story, while simultaneously hiding the true identities of the characters involved in the work (27). Allegory literally protects the writer and the audience's mortal lives in some cases (20,26).

Simply put, if you think you know what something means before you give yourself the time, space, and opportunity to learn, and meditate on the information for at least 1 day, you are a rube with hubris. The KJV Bible is also packed with double entendre (29). Double entendre is a word or phrase open to two interpretations, one of which could be interpreted as sexually indecent. If you don't give yourself the time for deep understanding through meditation, then the emotion pimps who push mass media disinformation propaganda have inherited your birthright (land) as their prize (30). The Bible story in Genesis dealing with Jacob and Esau is describing a mental war plain and simple. Failure to acknowledge this exacting truth will make you a candidate for the greatest deception the existing One, Jehovah Elohim ever constructed. Stymied for our benefit in my estimation. Identity theft? Jew who? Yew?

Ignorance is bliss when you hide behind your ego. Higo is Spanish for fig [leaf] (31). For the woke, ignorance is a place of mental punishing, indecision, and stiff-necked irrational anguish. Your egocentrism exposes the void in your calculations called gray area and F.E.A.R. (False Evidence Appearing Real). Should we call people like this Doubting

Thomas with Stockholm Syndrome? Maybe they're a Humpty Dumpty stuck on the fence, de-fense? I also like to think of this spiritual or intellectual void as the vacuum of hades to keep my land tilled properly. Adam from the Book of Genesis has always meant 'mankind', and Eve has always been defined as 'living' in the Hebrew or Aramaic used in the Bible's Old Testament advanced technology, mental math handbook (32). Cain is simply the unforgiving and jealous portion of your personality landscape. Cain appears to be the portion of our conscious thinking that rejects the [en]able[d] (Abel) or super ego part of our personality ménage trois, discovered by Sigmund Freud (33). His Psychoanalytic Theory is better known as the Id, the Ego, and the Superego (35,36). The so-called African American woman will prove Freud's theory to be exact beyond our wildest dreams (34).

3. The Real Secret Behind Why You Are Trapped in Egypt

Miser[y]aim or double straits best defines the actual symptoms of the mysterious Ancient Egypt mental mind state swamp. The term Miseraim or Egypt best describes the troubled waters of the left and right hemispheres (Upper and Lower respectively) of the brain in my humble estimation (37). Denial or D' Nile (French) are the corrupted waters of your mind whilst in the mental state of Egypt or Miseraim. The mental structure that is built up on the mental mindscape is called Egypt, which is a bipyramidal structure or octahedron (The Sims emerald gem maybe?) (38,39). Egypt can also mean boxed-in by willful selfishness, rendering you an automated (triggerable; trigonometry) mental bondage box-troll zombie (40).

One of my favorite anthropological examples of the, 'Automated Mental Bondage Box-Troll Zombie' to study is the poor Christian/European colonists as they pulled themselves out of poverty and squalor from the Antebellum period, to the post-Civil War Reconstruction Era from 1789-1900 (41,43). The poor white's willingness to obey his corporate federalist banking masters (Crown Corporation) was unprecedented during this period in American history (42). Later, Jim Crow and the Black Codes were laws that were created by these former Europeans out of this time-period (44). Most of the laws passed in the latter part of the 19th century, were created to favor the rich white industrialist class, as well as facilitate the ambitions of Black Top Hat wearing Jewish Zionist federalist corporate bankster land pirates. Flash a mental image of the mascot for the Monopoly board game. Yes, the little Zionist man with the Black top hat and bigoté [1984]. Wealthy landowning whites, and their bootlicking fearful self-interested servants, should properly be called the American Nobel Class for exacting purposes.

The competition for employment and control of land use was fierce during the late 1800s. Whites did not want to economically compete with the newly freed negro slaves, let alone any of the other European immigrant groups who intended on colonizing the Americas (Moreno Bey). White labor unions like the Klu Klux Klan resorted to political violence (terrorism) to prevent other racial groups from prospering (45,48). The white American Nobel did everything conceivable to secure positions of power in North America up to and including: religious persecutions, poisonings, arson, rape, castrations, murders, political assassinations, bombings, drive-by shootings, guerilla tactics, terrorist threats up to and equaling acts of genocide (46).

'Yellow Journalism' is America's first effective Fake News. 'Yellow Journalism', historically, has caused angry mobs of white men took take the "law" into their own hands. 'Yellow Journalism' has incited white men to lynch and beat Negroes and Indians. Many of the photos we see of Black men and women being hanged from trees like Christmas ornaments throughout the 20th century was caused by 'Yellow Journalism'. The original silent film, The Birth of a Nation (1915), was first released and screened in the White House by then United States President Woodrow Wilson (D). President Wilson was a devout Democrat and proud Klu Klux Klansman. This film was used as a recruiting/motivational video for the KKK. It is an example of effective 'Yellow Journalism'. Is the modern movie, The Birth of a Nation (2016), a modern-day example of

'Yellow Journalism'? Is this new movie an attempt to make African Americans and other minority groups more prone to commit violent acts against modern White Americans? The children haven't been given an opportunity to compare the two movies. Most American parents don't even know that the 1915 film exists.

It's important to note that the addition of the 14th Amendment to the U.S. Constitution in 1868 was not intended to aid or assist the so-called Negros, Latinos, or Asians (44,46). The problem is the hidden in language. The 14th Amendment created an assumption of tangible evidence called prima facie (49). Basically, this allows perverts in corporate venues to create word-salads for the intentional purpose of coloring (tincturing) judicial opinions. Language coloring and coding are Masonic (Jedi) magical mind tricks to place you willingly under the rule of land barons, wordsmiths, and sexual malcontents, willingly.

Mitt Romney, former governor of Massachusetts, and U.S. presidential candidate in 2012, is strangely famous for saying that "corporations are people my friends" (56). He Freudian slipped up and admitted to the world the 'open' secret that corporations are 'persons', dead persons, or corpus delecti under the 14th Amendment (49,52,53,55). Supposedly, we are Vessels lost at sea (54). These language leaps are essential to the elitist globalist wordsmith circle jerkers like the Scriveners, Vatican City, Square Mile, and Washington, D.C. corporations respectively. Super PACs or political action committees, are now known as U.S. citizens on paper, with the same 'Constitutionally' (circa 1878) protected rights to use 'their' money as 1st Amendment protected 'political speech', e.g., buying advertising time just like you and I as living human souls (58). Does Citizen's

United ring your ole cracked liberty bell?

The Organization Man is a book that was published in 1956. This novel examines the character traits and tendencies of the white European colonists and their offspring as they were being transformed from farmers into the 'company man', a highly paid corporate hoary type (57). The 'company man' has a mentality that comes outfitted with backwards racial thinking, constant bootlicking, money grubbing avarice, and get-a-long to get-a-long nature that must have made their grandfathers and grandmothers turn to dust prematurely, in their graves and mausoleums from the continual rotations in full repugnance. Good corporate jobs include employers like the city, state, and federal governments. The military, defense contracting, and the aerospace industry are also examples of highly paid corporate jobs. The 'Big 3' car manufactures like Ford, Chevrolet, and Chrysler should have immediately surfaced on your forehead: Your brain is the Real Magic 8-ball. Say this phrase 3 times. Believe it, and you will be cured from the curse of Ancient Egypt (ignorance).

"I am on top of my squared cube, not trapped inside of my squared cube."

Language historically, has been used as a trap (59). Jacob's ladder was probably manufactured from hemp like the U.S. Constitution was. If you plan on climbing 'out' of ignorance, don't think you won't have to climb. YHWH Elohim made the cloud to protect the Israelites who were travelling out of Egypt. The internet is called the Cloud (Nephle[m]) too right? Oh, just checking your cheeky.

Brain Theory 528…Imagine this, what if the outcomes in our lives were based on our relative knowledge of the definitions of the words we used every day. Every life event could be compared to the visual experiences of examining the picture quality of your television screen. Now, mentally focus on the image quality specifically. Low Def=Low Clarity, High in Definitions=High Clarity; Low Visual Instruction=Low Mental Performance Capabilities, High Minded Instruction=Higher Quality Mental Performance Possibilities.

Are learning definitions more important than drinking water? I do not believe I can find words strong enough to drive home the importance of words, as well as their relative definitions (60). Maybe 9-inch nails through Jesus' wrists will do? Definitions are instructions. Ask any Hebrew/Aramaic scholar or teacher. Married together, definitions and the inherit corresponding instructions, are more important today to humanity than any other nuclear reaction ever contrived or tested.

The following paragraph will be used to reveal another 'open' secret/mystery that every English reader, speaker, or teacher should keep in mind always: Word phonetics stay the same, but the definitions of those words are what have been changed overtly (61). Definition/instruction word comprehension is the rug that has been pulled out from underneath all of humanity. Etymology is a latent science of fiction dialectic in itself. All English words have architecture. English words are spelled and organized in accordance with the rules of grammar. In [the queen's] English, words stay the same (20). The definitions are what have been very prudently changed over the centuries and decades. Most people live their whole life never knowing this fundamental queerness of the modern

English tongue, along with its many dialects including legalese. Legalese is an English dialect that is used for civil actions in legislation, contracts, banks or courts. At this stage in human brain evolution, the necessity of knowing multiple definitions of multitudes of words from different reference sources, and language scripts is paramount.

The Science of Fiction Dialectic gives Einstein's Unified Field Theory an opportunity to be tested again (61). This white boy's Theory of Relativity should also be applied to as many topics as you can think up, spanning all light beams at the same time. This process will feel like you are learning a new language because you are. Please research the corporate nation-state called the 'City of London' or 'Square Mile'. This body politic of world financial dominance is often confused with the corporate municipality or city named London. There are distinct differences between the two corporate entities.

The need for a violent strong man, dictator, tyrant, democrat, or despot to burn books, scrolls, and other vital historical records is no longer needed when the populace is unable to read the documents and symbols that are right in front of their faces every day. To find out the extent of the trickery infesting our institutions of higher learning, please research the origins of the Frankfurt School, and the O. S. S. or the Office of Strategic Service. The Frankfurt school is a group of Marxists defectors who came to America from Germany during the rise of Nazi fascism circa 1933 (62). The Frankfurt School academics are direct contributors to the current weakened state of the higher education system, and is the root cause of most of its structural failures (64,65). The Frankfurt School, via their mechanized zombie professor activists, pushed 'Political Correctness' down America's collective throat (67). The OSS's founding and covert information gathering techniques, lead to it be rebranded as the now infamous, Central Intelligence Agency (CIA). John Foster Dulles and his little brother Alan Welsh Dulles, are the filthy gringos (Anglo-Americans) who are responsible for the violent overthrows of many Central and South American nations (66). Their mission was to topple governments (finance national overthrows) for the sole purpose of profit and commodities control. This plan stemmed from the Monroe Doctrine. The Monroe Doctrine, outlined by the United States, was a plan to strategically apply economic/military controls over the western hemisphere, waterways included. The greatest book you can find to fully understand the intricacies of U.S. foreign policy coming out of WW2, is Confessions of an Economic Hit Man (2004), written by the economic hit-man/negotiator himself, John Perkins.

Nazi 'Political Correctness' tactics were and are still used to this day. 'Political Correctness' was used to smart the minds of America's Greatest Generation, those born from the 1920's to 1945 (65,67). The Baby Boomer generation are the sheeple crops of Americans who were hatched from 1946 to1964. This group received their 'Political Correctness' training not only from their socially traumatized and war drum deafened parents, but also from the rest of their intoxicated village, including the paranoid and superstitious church circles from generations before. 'Political Correctness' programming can also be found in the interactions of secretive fraternity and sorority groups, K-12 social engineering curriculums, and radio and television waves, the other smart bomb 'programming'. Today, all other American generations suffer because of these vast information gaps that were created and sealed by this well-orchestrated Majestik-12, Gray Alien magical mind trick (68). I would like to thank you Dr. Michael Savage for your wisdom and spiritual guidance over the years on radio. His vital intelligence perspective on the fascists of the Frankfurt School made it possible for me to see clearly. U.F.O.s are out there, folks! Look up! Did I just see a drone?

Those of us who have been lucky enough to go to college, have at some time, attempted to sell our textbooks back to the college bookstore. The reason why you may have not been able to sell the books back, is due to a very familiar phenomenon called the re-vision. Information, critical to understanding exactly where humans are or have been in relation to our societal evolution is either intentionally left out, or 'Politically Corrected' to the point of neutering and distorting the critical Zeit Geist messages of that time (69). Global Climate Change is a great example of the truth and a lie. A 'Consensus' exists in climate science circles, that global warming is "man-made" global climate change, because of climate data that is accepted based only on the credentials of its authors. They have failed to fully disclose exactly what 'climate' is warming, or what exactly is 'man-made' about the so-called changes. Whose climate is warming? Is it like an older woman's menopause warming? [idk]

The next time you pick up a book or dictionary, look for the edition or version it is, and look for its publishing date. Just like wine, the older the text the easier it will be to get the gist of what is being presented based on the minds of the people who would have been reading it at the time it was published.

It's time for you to start thinking like Dr. Evil in a blue dress. Even though you will suffer from this type of mindset, imagine that you are the absolute worst savage dictator princess alive. You are a woman who hates human beings so much that you regularly arrange for their sacrificial murders, as well as the ritual torture and rape of small children. The prudence behind the brutality and blood shed, would be to keep the population in your colony under your control through pure fear. At the same time, feeding your wicked mercenary army with debauchery and plunder, while you indulge on your own bizarre thirst for children's blood. Now imagine your ambitions eventually lead you to dream up an idea to change mankind's perception of their own history. It has been found that all you would have to do is change the way your subject's hormones release when they are presented with new information, situations or circumstances (73). Normalcy Bias and Cognitive Dissonance Theory together work great at helping to explain why the human brain rejects well founded conspiracy theories, as well as great Greek tragedy (70).

"Normalcy Bias is Food Preference." (Judith Jones).

Those who fail to comprehend the past, and the origins of the language being used in whatever they are reading, will settle for any perverted historical nonsense (71). Biased wordsmithing, coupled with the use of relentless physical force and racial (class) segregation, would allow you to control the colonists within your democracy. 'Political Correctness' is a symbol of utter weakness in a free republic of free speech lovers. Your mind is the only time machine you will ever need or know. The use of well written books and vintage black and white movies from America's early 20th century, will be perfect training aides for any time-travel expedition. Albert Pike, the founder of the KKK agrees, symbols are more powerful than words (72).

The blind, tell people that they are 'dumbed down' without knowing that they are 'dumbed down' too. The phrase 'dumbing down the next generation', simply means quieting their natural instincts (i.e., their ability to ask a question, see, and call bullshit), and cause those around them to disregard their outcry as invalid and baseless due to their own ignorance. Most people are filled with their own brand of socially engineered selfishness, self-doubt, and unquenched suspicion. The children in America see the adults around them as the weak push-overs they have been bred to become (75). We must listen to and engage with the children on 'their' level because they're not fully brainwashed. Young people are simply egocentric subjects of their own mirror neuro-chemicals.

Expecting the 'know-it-all' types of people to make time to consider your observations may be close to impossible without finding a way to show them that their skin is in this game too. Yes, this that we currently call reality is literally a game outfitted with penal codes, tax penalties, and biased referees (judges).

Here's a question to ask yourself for the rest of the day, 'would you be willing to listen to you'? Saying this phrase in front of a mirror will cure your shyness, and give you holy boldness. Meditate on this commonly known and misunderstood maxim for the next 21 days, 'deaf, dumb, and blind'. What d'angers were the scholars in American academic circles trying to warn us about by giving Americans the story of Helen Keller? What's ironic is that most Americans are real life Hellen Kellers: robotic sheeple who are functionally deaf, dumb, and blind to the occult (hidden). American apathy and ignorance has created generations of people who are totally unable to speak lucidly, see clearly, or even hear the vital information concerning multitudes of important topics coming at them every day from varying mediums, their own intellect included.

We must know that knowledge naturally builds on itself. This is, in my opinion, detrimental to increasing the capacity of our collective brain intelligibility, and its conscious evolution. Most of us are not the critical thinkers our Father (Greek for Pater[n]) in heaven intended us to be yet. The strong among us are stymied by the power of this massive deception we call life, liberty, and the pursuit of happiness, which is simply avarice masked by our collective tendencies toward blissful ignorance while mirroring the actions and deeds of our collective oppressors. This appears to be simple human ignorance to elementary quantum physics enthusiasts like myself. Our confusion was a planned psychological, military, religious, and mathematical operation of the oldest kind (74,75).

I may be the only Moor on the Earth who believes that the clay tablets of the Ancient Sumerians (excavated in Iraq circa 1851-52), Madam Blavatsky, and Sigmund Freud have all contributed to the rise of modern psychology and mass marketing. Madam Helena Blavatsky is world famous for creating the Theosophy Society in the 1870s. Madam Blavatsky's work was also the inspiration behind Alice and Foster Bailey's founding of World Goodwill and the Lucis Trust, a registered 501(c) 3 since 1922. The original name of this Non-Profit was the Lucifer Trust (76). The name was changed in 1923 for obvious reasons, but what isn't so obvious is that the Lucis Trust is the publishing company for the useless United Nations. The Bill and Melinda Gate's Foundation gives your donation money to the Lucis Trust as a sub-corporation. The Bill and Melinda Gate's Foundation also contributes financially to Planned Parenthood, the baby murderers and baby body parts farmers. Facts.

The Bilderberg Group was formed by Jewish Zionist world banking elite cross dressing pedophile weirdos in 1953 to destroy the American white middle class. The Federal Board of Education was then created as a United States corporate institution in 1954 to keep the children trapped in a dream-like reality, while the bankers continued to rob the nation of its true wealth: the human's mental faculties and natural abilities (75). Any honest American with 'Pre-Internet Age' knowledge will agree that academic scholarship in America has suffered a sharp decline overall since the1950's. Here is one possible reason: Satan inspired government psychological operations [Church military outposts included] are real and all around us. United States Army General Michael Akino should be a household name to every so-called freedom loving American, and Oprah Winfrey fan. General Akino worked for the U.S. Army as a Green Beret psychological operations specialist. The U.S. Army knew he was a worshipping Satanist. He is a master of psychological military operations, and has worked for the United States Army from 1968 to recent years. During his military career, he was charged with at least one indecent sexual act with minor. He was one of the first Army officers to be put in charge of the NSA. If you didn't already know, the National Security Agency keeps America safe by capturing and storing our cell phone call data, text messages, and metadata, but that's ok, right? No one is going to listen later, right? I vvonder vvhat evil deeds the NSA may have retrieved on U.S. Supreme Court Justice John Roberts to retard his decision-making ability in 2010 when it came to the Obamacare/Healthcare Reform Act (77). The Obamacare legislation mysteriously transformed into a tax, and not a law, as many Americans and state legislators had expected it to be. Ironically, the healthcare bill calls for the funding on a small army. This well-regulated army corps will be under the direct control of the executive branch (H.R. 3590 Patient Protection & Affordable Care Act 3/23/2010).

Whether you like to admit it, all the material "anything" you ever desired or worked hard for is the prudent outcome of a grand deception: your own precept-ion of desire over necessity. The transmitting of the television and radio waves into our homes was the single greatest achievement of these aggressive, pansexual, 'spirit pimping', capitalist oligarchs. The 'Illuminators' use our 'free will' by influencing and manipulating our unconscious animal mind (id) to do things that when one becomes 'spiritually' awakened to the manipulation, one becomes physically ill to the gravity of what they had been manipulated or hypnotized to do, think, say, feel and believe. 12 years a slave? 20 years on the J. O. B. ("Just Over Broke"-Frank and Patty in Oxnard) or maybe 40 years of dedicated robotic employment?

During times of deep contemplation, Normalcy Bias and Cognitive Dissonance theory can be triggered, preventing a true awakening from unfolding on the subconscious, neurological, alchemical, and subsequently hormonal/biological levels (70). All historically significant Klu Klux Klan members were Democrats. Presidential hopeful

Bernie Sanders (D) supported the Southern Poverty Law Center during his run in 2016. The SPLC has protected KKK members since 1961. The Federal Bureau of Investigation washed their hands of the SPLC in January of 2014. The SPLC supported President Obama's (D) presidency. They also supported legislation and fear tactics that tried to take gun ownership rights away from young African American men and women. Facts. Fuck Bernie Sanders (D), and Fuck the Southern Poverty Law Center! I became an Oath Keeper out of respect for the brave and beguiled men and women who served us honorably in the U.S. military, and in varying law enforcement capacities. I would have never met these brave Americans if I didn't say to myself, "Fuck the SPLC" in October 2009. I, intellectually, was 7 years ahead of presidential hopeful Bernie Sanders, with his floppy misguided existence. He is the model American Democrat boxed-troll demon. Alex Jones and Stewart Rhodes, I thank you for the interview on Infowars.com you two did a week or so before the Oath Keepers' 1st Annual Conference in Las Vegas, Nevada in October 2009. I was in attendance. I have 2 white guys to thank for what I think is my sanity. [One]

Components of Particles

The Science of Fiction Dialectic Sources List

<u>These Particles are Containers:</u> Each Particle includes anything that can be called data. Data can be found in website servers, books, documentaries, lexicons, dictionaries, encyclopedias, Wikipedia for live research efforts, professional experience, etc.

Components of Particle 1

1. Book: Christie, Richard. Geis, Florence L. *Studies in Machiavellianism.* Academic Press. 1970; Google books. 2013.

2. "Official"; definition: *Black's Law Dictionary (1891), 6th Edition.* West Publishing. 1990.

3. "Comforter"; definition: *The New Strong's Exhaustive Concordance of the Bible.* Thomas Nelson. 2009.

4. Lengua; Spanish definition; https://www.merriam-webster.com/dictionary/Lengua;

5. Rubric; definition; https://www.google.com/#q=rubric+definition;

6. Discern; definition; http://www.dictionary.com/browse/discern;

7. Reprobate; definition; http://www.biblestudytools.com/dictionary/reprobate/;

8. "Catching the Holy Ghost,". The thought power of the Word mixed with passion can make people eat grass. It happed in South Africa in 2014: http://www.dailymail.co.uk/news/article-2537053/Lawn-Christians-South-African-preacher-makes-congregation-eat-GRASS-closer-God.html,

9. You Tube video of South African Grass-eating Church-goers (2014): https://www.youtube.com/watch?v=IPDL331eNVI;

10. Scholarly article on Zombies; Nasiruddin, M. Halabi, M. Dao, A. Chen, K. Brown, B. *Zombies: A Pop Culture Resource for Public Health Awareness.* CDC Emerging Infectious Diseases Journal Vol. 19, Number 5. 2013.

https://wwwnc.cdc.gov/eid/article/19/5/ad-1905_article

11. Scholarly article on Sympathetic and Parasympathetic Nervous Systems;

Glick, G. Braunwald, E. Lewis, R. *Relative Roles of the Sympathetic and Parasympathetic Nervous Systems in the Reflex Control of Heart Rate.* American Heart Association Journal. 1965.

http://circres.ahajournals.org/content/16/4/363;

12. Mirror Neurons scholarly article:

Iacoboni, Marco. *Imitation, Empathy, and Mirror Neurons.* Annual Review of Psychology, Vol. 60:653-670. 2009
http://annualreviews.org/doi/abs/10.1146/annurev.psych.60.110707.163604,

13. Scholarly article: [Are] Humans are different from monkeys?

Heyes, Cecilia. *Where Do Mirror Neurons Come From?* Neuroscience & Behavioral Reviews, Vol. 43, Issue 4. 2010.

http://www.sciencedirect.com/science/article/pii/S0149763409001730;

14. Sensorimotor Stage; definition is on the web page;
http://web.cortland.edu/andersmd/PIAGET/sms.HTML; or Cherry, Kendra. *What is the Sensorimotor Stage of Cognitive Development?* (July 12, 2017). https://www.verywell.com/sensorimotor-stage-of-cognitive-development-2795462

15. 1st Corinthians, XIV.19, King James Version Bible verse (1769);

16. All Law is Based on Water:

Schoenbaum, T. McClellan, J. *Admiralty and Maritime Law 5th Edition.* West publishing. 2012; books.google.com.

17. Did Organic laws exist before Organic food? Yes.

Thorpe, Francis Newton. *THE FEDERAL AND STATE CONSTITUTIONS: COLONIAL CHARTERS, AND OTHER ORGANIC LAWS OF THE STATES, TERRITORIES, AND COLONIES,*

NOW AND HEREFORE FORMING THE UNITED STATES OF AMERICA. Washington. Printing Office. 1909.; FN Thorpe-1909-books.google.com;

18. Shorter, Edward. *From Paralysis to Fatigue: A History of Psychosomatic Illness in the Modern Era.* Free Press. 1992. books.google.com.

Components of Particle 2

19. Berry, Lloyd Eason. *The Geneva Bible: A Facsimile of the 1560 Edition.* Hendrickson Publishers. 2007; books.google.com.

20. Scholarly article on Queen Elizabeth's Battle of the Bibles:

Betteridge, Maurice S. The Bitter Notes: The Geneva Bible and Its Annotations. The Sixteenth Century Journal Vol. 14, No. 1. (1983).

21. English-Semitic roots, RB Kaplan - Language learning, 1966 - Wiley Online Library;

22. Semitic/English Comparative Dictionary of Ge'ez, Wolf Leslau - 1987 - books.google.com;

23. Commercial Banks origins: Dean F. Amel - Board of Governors, unpublished paper, September, 1993 - fraser.stlouisfed.org

24. *Base Ball and the Rule of Law / Mayflower Compact:* Finkelman, Paul A., (1998)

25. *Electrophysiology Evidence for Two Steps in & Syntactic Analysis: Early Automatic and Late Controlled Process (Cognitive Neuroscience).* 1999. Hahne, Anja. Friederici, Angela D. (Max Planck Inst.): http://www.mitpressjournals.org/doi/abs/10.1162/089892999563328#.WO7ntNLyvIU

26. Allegory; definition: JanMohamed, Abdul R. *The Economy of Manichean Allegory: The Function of Racial Difference in Colonialist Literature.* University of California, Berkley. 1985.

27. Scholarly article: Belting, Hans. University of Munich. *The Role of Narrative in Public Painting of the Trecento: "Historia" and Allegory.* 1985.

28. Allegory definition: https://en.oxforddictionaries.com/definition/allegory

29. Scholarly article: Lefcourt, Herbert M. Gronnerud, Paul. McDonald, Peter. *Cognitive Activity and Hypothesis Formation During Double Entendre*

Word Association Test as a Function of Locus Control and Field Dependence. Canadian Journal of Behavioural Science. 1972.

30. Prize definition: Thayer Greek Lexicon. G1017; **brabeion** [bribe]; used only 2 times in the KJV; 1 Corinthians 9:24 and Philippians 3:14.

31. Higo [fig tree] definition: http://www.wordreference.com/es/en/translation.asp?spen=higo

32. The Hebrew lengua is also called Aramaic: (1995) New Strong's Concordance (KJV) Concise Dictionary for words in the Hebrew Bible.

(See Introduction pages, i and ii).

33. Ménage à trois; [Nicki Minaj] definition for educational and double entendre purposes; https://www.merriam-webster.com/dictionary/m%C3%A9nage%20%C3%A0%20trois

34. Scholarly article on psychoanalytic theory for Moorish American Women; Rosen, H. Zickler, E. 1996. *Feminist Psychoanalytic Theory: American and French reactions to Freud.* Journal of American Psychoanalytic Association.

35. Fenichel, Otto and Rangell, Leo M.D. *The Psychoanalytic theory of Neurosis.* 1945

36. Scholarly article: Hartman, Heinz M.D. *Comments On The Psychoanalytic Theory of Ego [*].* Journal: The Psychoanalytic Study of the Child. 1950. [*] Read the Convention of the American Psychoanalytic Association in Montreal, May, 1949.
http://www.tandfonline.com/doi/abs/10.1080/00797308.1950.11822886?journalCode=upsc20

Components of Particle 3

37. H4714. Egypt or Miseraim (see pronunciation in Strong's Concordance for the secret phonetics); Upper and Lower Egypt; dual of H4693 (māṣôr)- Egypt (as the border of Palestine); H4692 in the sense of a limit; something hemming in, i.e. a mound, (abstractly) a siege, (figuratively) distress, (subjectively) a fatness; etymology root: from H6696, to cramp. i.e., confine (in many applications, literally or figuratively, formative or hostile).

38. Duffey, George H. 1950. *Bipyramidal Heptacovalent Bonds Orbitals.* Journal of Chemical Physics 18, 943. AIP Publishing.

http://aip.scitation.org/doi/abs/10.1063/1.1747815

39. Fujii, Hiroshi. Funahashi, Yasuhiro. *A Triagonal-Bipyramidal Ferric Aqua Complex with a Sterically Hindered Salen Ligand as a Model for the Active Site of Protocatechuate 3, 4-Dioxygenas.* 2002. Angewandte Chemie. http://onlinelibrary.wiley.com/doi/10.1002/1521-3773(20021004)41:19%3C3638::AID-ANIE3638%3E3.0.CO;2-%23/full

40. English phrase: Boxed in; definition: Cambridge Dictionary, http://dictionary.cambridge.org/us/dictionary/english/boxed-in

41. Antebellum; definition: Occurring or existing before a war; i.e., the history of America before the Civil War 1859-1864.

https://en.oxforddictionaries.com/definition/antebellum

42. Websdale, Julian. October 2013. *The Crown Empire and the City of London Corporation.* https://wakeup-world.com/2013/11/05/the-crown-empire-and-the-city-of-london-corporation/; World Freemasonry exposed;

Additional source for the origins of all corporations; You Tube video: Luciferian Crown Empire, Crown Temple, City of London Corporation, Jesuit Merchants [The Order of the Garter]. You Tube channel: Emancipated by TRUTH. https://www.youtube.com/watch?v=_IB15IE1JC0

43. Sullivan, Barry. *Historical Reconstruction, Reconstruction History, and the Proper Scope of Section 1981.* The Yale Law Journal Company. 1989. Volume 98, No. 3.
http://www.jstor.org/stable/796629?seq=1#page_scan_tab_contents; http://www.jstor.org/stable/796629

44. Alexander, Michelle. *The New Jim Crow: Mass incarceration in the Age of Colorblindness*. The New Press. 2012.

45. <u>Origins of Unions and Antisemitism</u>:

Arendt, Hannah. *The Origins of Totalitarianism, Part 1*. Houghton Mifflin Hartcourt. 1973.

46. Genocide scholarly article: Cooper, Leo. *Genocide: It's Political Use in the 20th century*. 1981. Yale University Press.

47. Book on Genocide: Lifton, Robert J. *The Nazi Doctors: The Medical Killing and the Psychology of Genocide*. 1986. Basic Books.

48. Scholarly article: Taylor, Robert. *Out of the Bowels of the Movement: The Trade Unions and the Origins of the Labour Party 1900-1918*. 2000. The Labour Party. Springer Link.
https://link.springer.com/chapter/10.1057/9780230595583_2

49. How does Prima Facie apply to my everyday life?; definition: Latin, "On Its Face" http://dictionary.law.com/Default.aspx?selected=1598

50. Gordon, Milton Myron. *Assimilation in American Life: The Role of Race, Religion, and National Origins*. Oxford University Press. 1964.
https://books.google.com/books?id=8KBHDAAAQBAJ&dq=origins+of+unions&lr=&source=gbs_navlinks_s

51. Scholarly article: Perman, Michael. Foner, Eric. *Review: Eric Foner's: Reconstruction: A Finished Revolution: Reconstruction: America's Unfinished Revolution, 1863-1877*. Harper and Row. The Johns Hopkins University Press. 1988. 1989.

52. Amar, Akhil Reed. *The Bill of Rights and the Fourteenth Amendment*. Yale Law School Faculty Scholarship Repository. 1992.

53. Corporations, persons, or individuals are the same; definitions: Black Law Dictionary 6th Edition. West Publishing. 1990

54. Are you dead or alive? Dead at birth?

Cestui Que(SET-A-KAY) Vie Trust Act of 1666.
http://www.legislation.gov.uk/aep/Cha2/18-19/11

55. Corpus Delicti (de-lic-ti) definition. http://legal-dictionary.thefreedictionary.com/corpus+delicti

56. Mitt Romney let the cat out of the bag with this quote, "Corporations are people (persons) my friend." This statement was made on 8/11/2011 while Mr. Romney was on the road during his 2012 Presidential election campaign.

57. Whyte, William H. *The Organization Man*. Simon & Schuster. 1956.

58. Benson, Robert W. *The End of Legalese: The Game is Over*. N.Y.U. Law Review & Social Change 519. 1984-1985. http://heinonline.org/HOL/LandingPage?handle=hein.journals/nyuls13&div=26&id=&page=

59. Hill, Claire A. *Why Contracts Are Written in "Legalese"*. Chicago Kent Law Review 59. 2001-2002.

60. Fine, Arthur. Brown, Harvey R. *The Shaky Game: Einstein, Realism, and the Quantum Theory*. American Journal of Physics. 1988. Book reviewer and editor: Baierlein, Department of Physics, Wesleyan University. http://aapt.scitation.org/doi/10.1119/1.15540

61. Cassirer, Ernst. Swabey, W. C., Swabey, M. C. *Substance and Function and Einstein's Theory of Relativity*. Courier Corporation. 2004.

62. Martin, Jay. *The Dialectical Imagination: A History of the Frankfurt School and the Institute of Social Research*. University of California Press. 1973.

63. Aroto, Andrew. Gebhardt, Eike. Piccone, Paul. *The Essential Frankfurt School*. The Continuum Publishing Company. 1982.

64. Cowling, Mark. Martin, James. *Marx's Lumpen-proletariat and Murray's Underclass: Concept Best Abandoned*. Marx Eighteenth Brumaire: (Post) Modern Interpretations. London. 2002. http://icspt.uchicago.edu/papers/2002/cowling02.pdf

65. Griffin, Roger. *The Nature of Fascism*. Psychology Press. 1991.

66. John Foster Dulles quote. Newspaper headline: "Dulles in Rio". "The U.S. has no friends, only interests". New York Times. 1958.

67. Search terms: 'Political' 'Correctness' on Wikipedia.com; great article as of 4/18/2017.

68. President Harry Truman's: *Operation Majestic 12*. 1947. https://vault.fbi.gov/Majestic%2012

69. Zeit Geist; definition. https://en.oxforddictionaries.com/definition/zeitgeist; Based on ideas and beliefs.

70. Cognitive Dissonance Theory scholarly article: Chen, M. Keith. *Rationalization and Cognitive Dissonance: Do Choices Affect or Reflect Preferences?* Cowles Foundation Discussion Paper No. 1669. 2008. https://papers.ssrn.com/sol3/papers.cfm?abstract_id=1160268

71. Democracy defined by Dahl, Robert A. *Democracy and its Critics*. Yale University Press. 1989.

72. Pike, Albert. *Morals and Dogma of the Ancient and Accepted Scottish Rite Freemasonry.* 1871

73. Bank, Court, Seat, Island, and Judge mean the same thing in Black's Law Dictionary 6th Edition. 1990.

74. D' Angers. https://en.wikipedia.org/wiki/Angers. (see etymology; "Black City"); Possible origin for "Dangerous Speech"; Schenck v. United States (1919); Is it legal to shout "fire" in a crowded theater?;

75. Web article by Mr. Militant Negro. *The United States of America King Alfred Plan: The Extermination of Blacks in AmeriKKKa! Code-named: Rex 84*. 2015. https://themilitantnegro.com/2015/05/30/the-king-alfred-plan-rex-84/

76. Lucis Trust (Lucifer Trust circa 1922), non-profit, is the publishing company for the United Nations. https://www.lucistrust.org/about_us/history

77. March 23, 2010. *Affordable Care Act,* was signed by President Obama, President Trump administration now has access;

H.R. 3590; SEC. 5210. ESTABLISHING A READY RESERVE CORPS…appointed by the President…all times be subject to call to active duty.

78. Additional source for the cause of all Central and South American revolutions and civil unrest was Wall Street:

Perkins, John. Copyright. 2004. *CONFESSIONS of an ECONOMIC HIT MAN*. Penguin Group Publishing. First Plume Printing. 2006.

HUMANITY ONLY HAS ONE MATH PROBLEM TO DEAL WITH, THEIR OWN...

ELECTRO MAGNETIC FIELD VECTORING OF PSEUDO-ROTATED SUBLIMATED BIASES.

NOW REPLACE THE ROTATIONS WITH TRANSLATIONS.

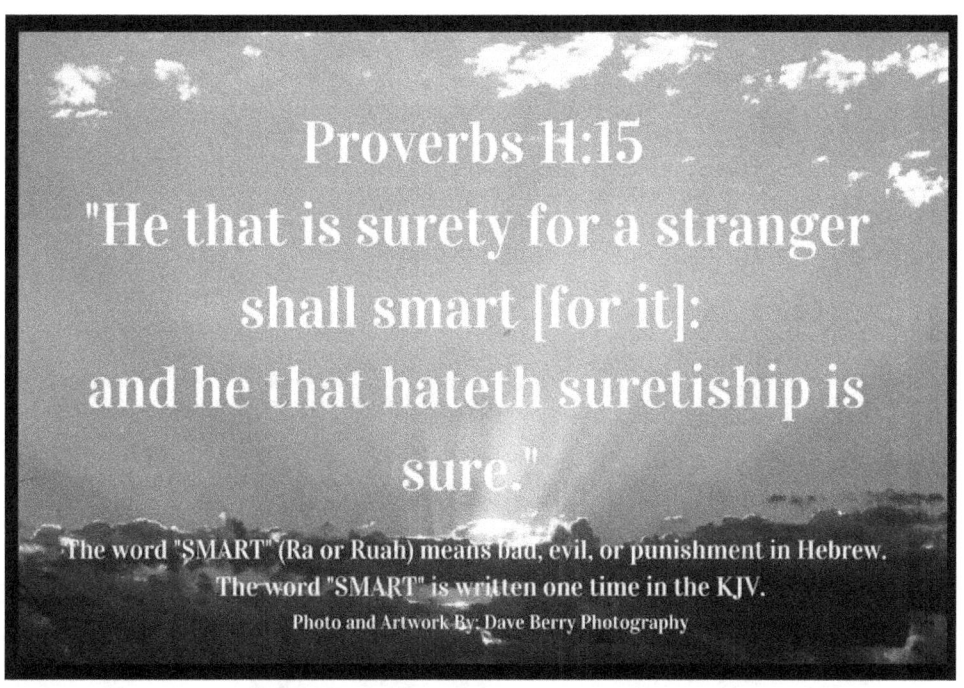

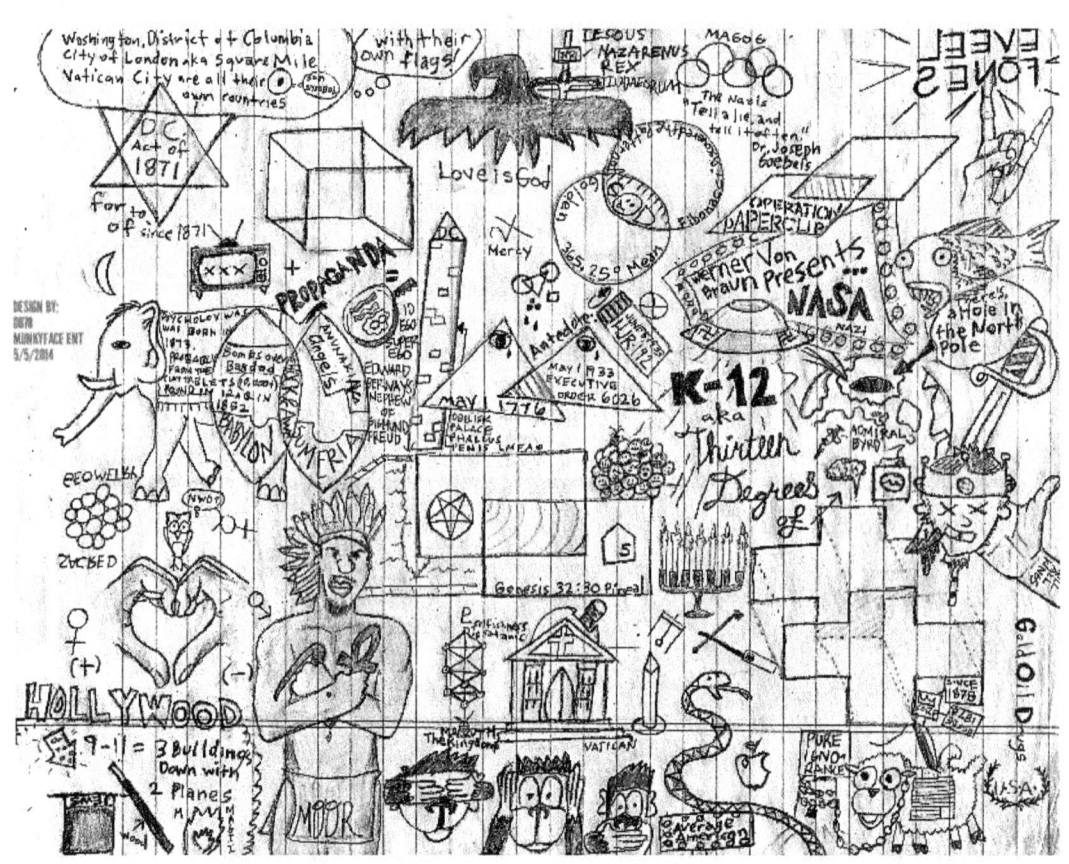

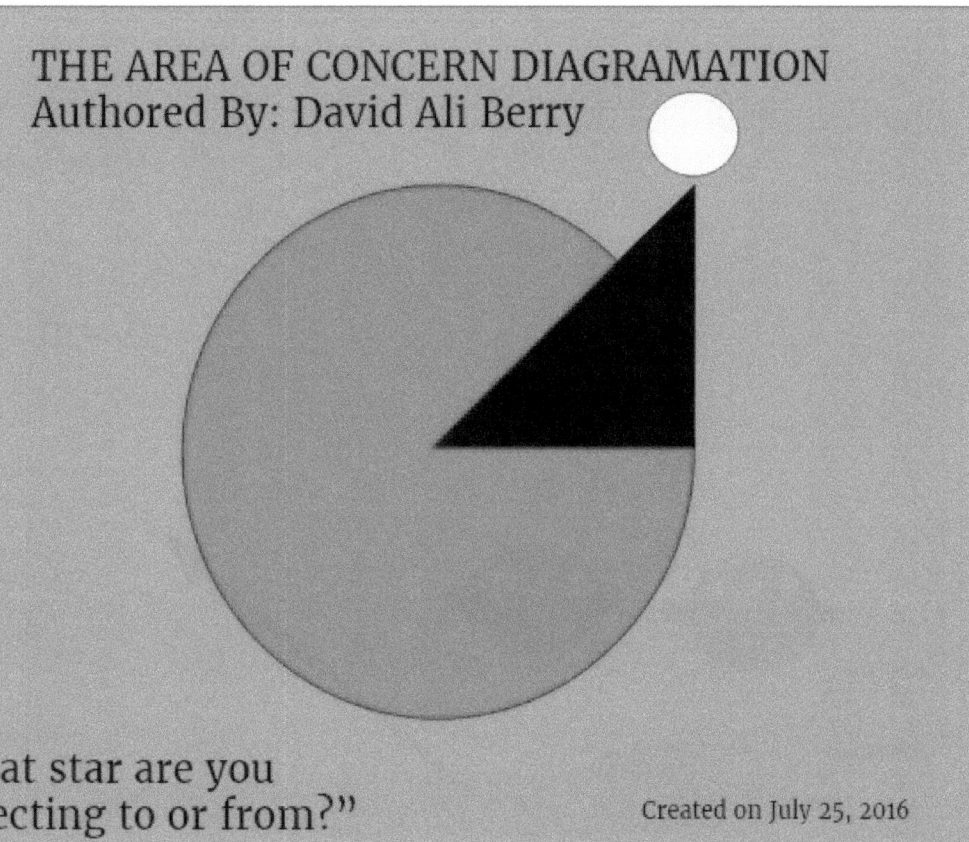

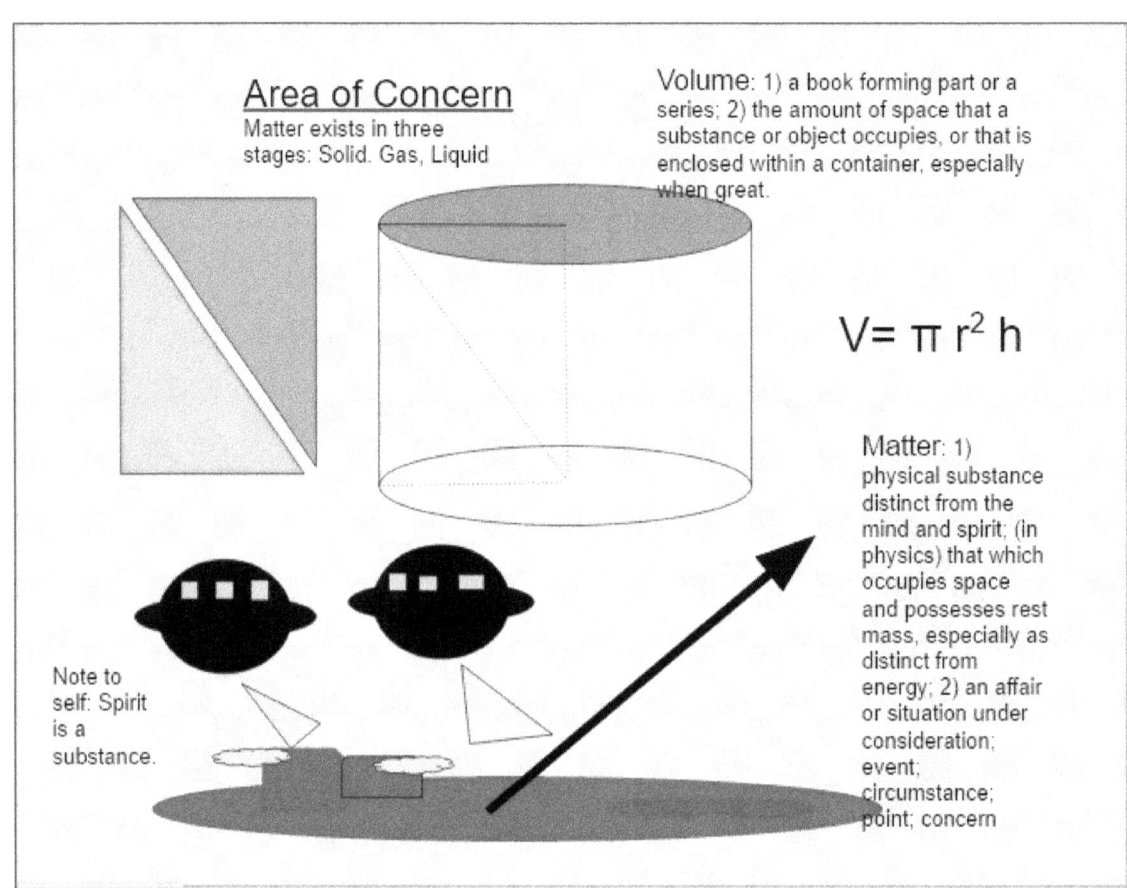

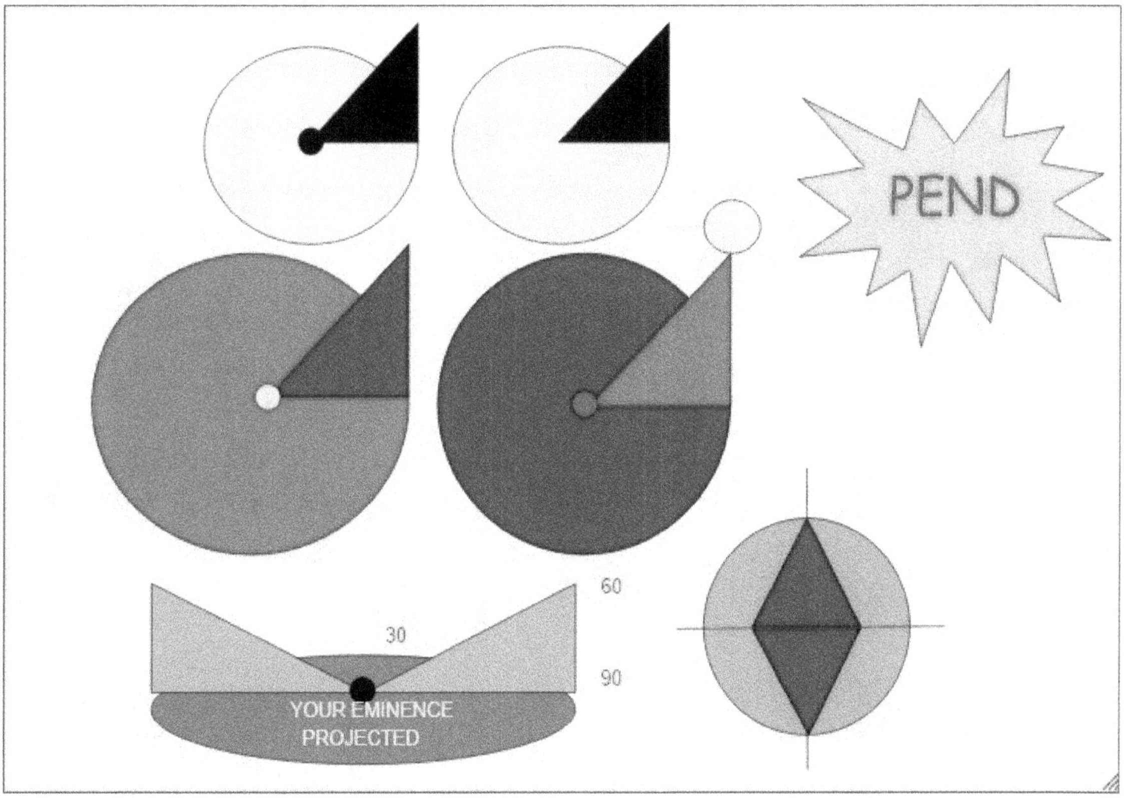

David Ali Berry EL

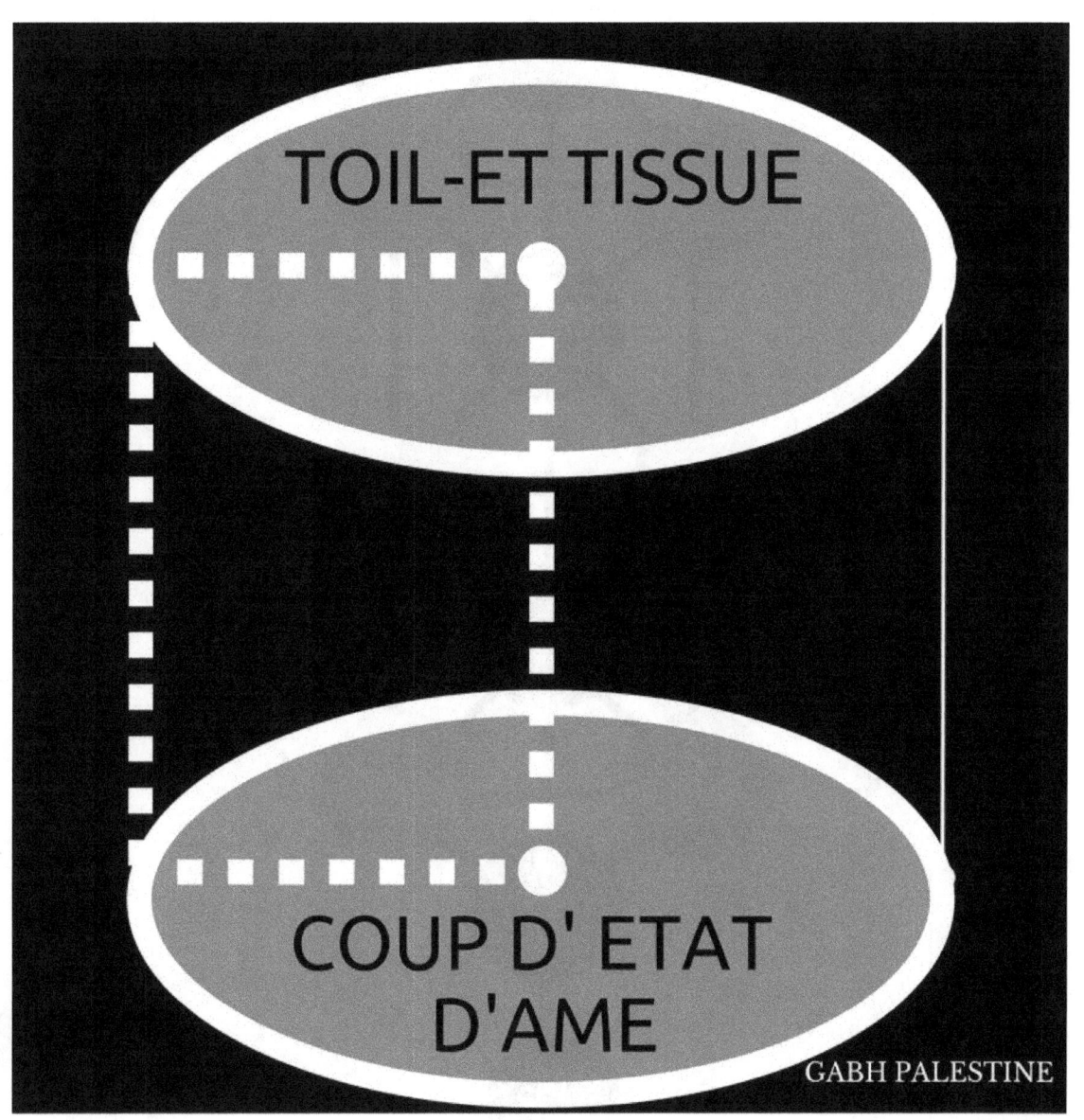

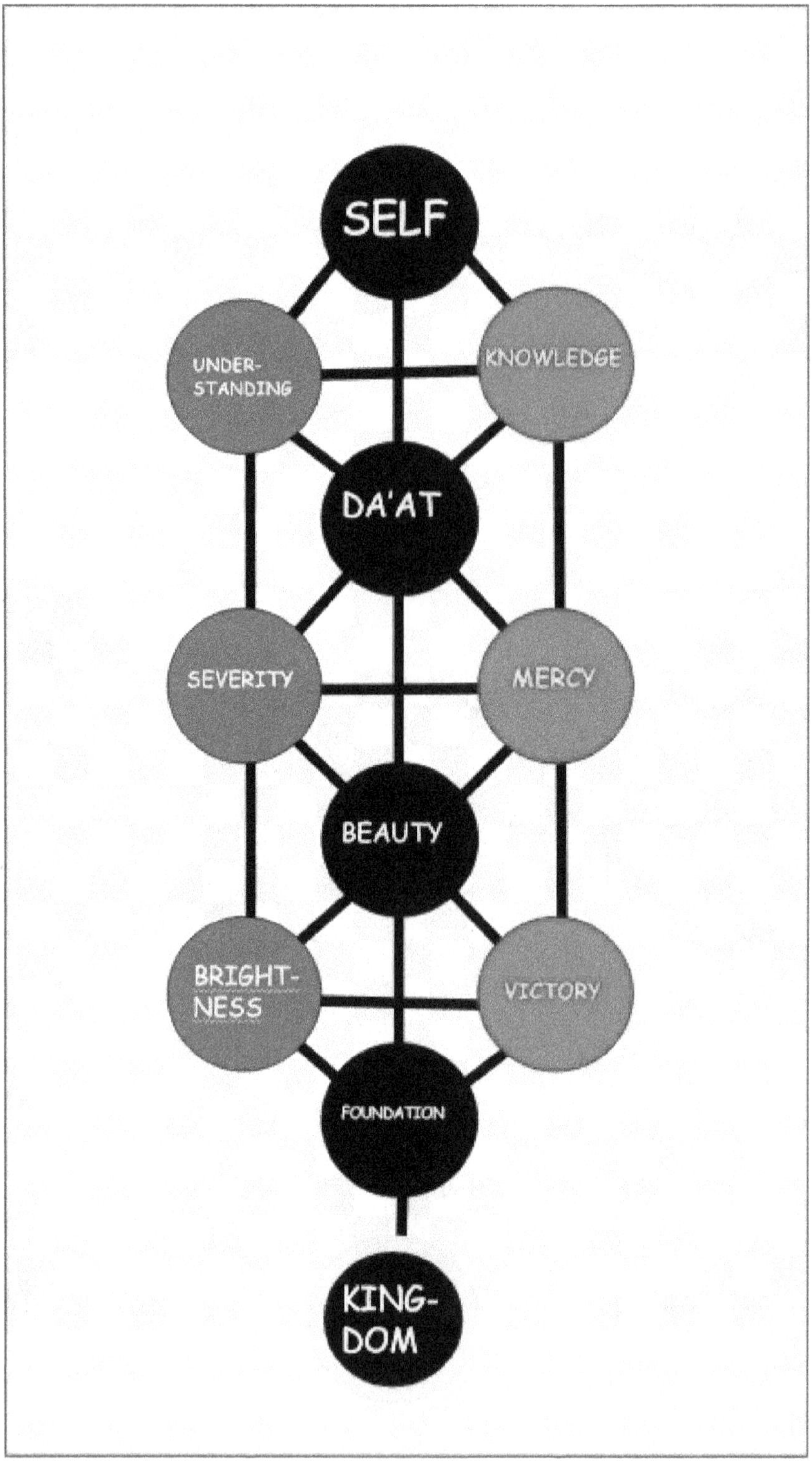
SELF
UNDER-
STANDING
KNOWLEDGE
DA'AT
SEVERITY
MERCY
BEAUTY
BRIGHT-
NESS
VICTORY
FOUNDATION
KING-
DOM

www.ingramcontent.com/pod-product-compliance
Lightning Source LLC
Chambersburg PA
CBHW081300170426
43198CB00017B/2859